MW01686982

The Lord's Prayer

Finding New Meanings Within the Language Jesus Spoke

The Lord's Prayer

Finding New Meanings Within the Language Jesus Spoke

PAUL W. MEIER

Published by Malcolm Creek Publishing,
Benton, KY 42025.

ISBN: 978-1-940424-07-1

Library of Congress PCN: 2015903336

* * *

To my wife, Barbara,

and the members of
St. Matthew by the Lake Lutheran Church
Benton, KY

for giving me the opportunity to study
and share what I learned
in my preparation for Sunday messages.

* * *

Acknowledgements:

I give special thanks and credit to the people who inspired this book and for their work in the interpretation of Aramaic texts.

In particular, The Nazarene Way of Essenic Studies, Neil Douglas-Klotz and his books dealing with interpretation of Aramaic texts: *Prayers of the Cosmos: Reflections on the Original Meaning of Jesus's Words* (HarperOne, 1993), that provided many of the poetic and imaginative phrases I list in this book. His website is www.abwoon.com. Another version of the Lord's Prayer was received from Rev. G.J. Ouseley who wrote *The Gospel of the Holy Twelve* (Dodo Press).

Other books by Paul W. Meier

The Beatitudes: Finding New Meanings in the Language Jesus Spoke

Praying the Gospels with Martin Luther: Finding Freedom in Love

How to Love the Lord Your God With All Your Heart and Change Your Life Forever

30 Days To Loving God With All Your Heart

The Kingdom of Heaven Begins Today

Divorce and Remarriage: Biblical Proof in Favor of Compassion

The ANCIENT Understanding of Eternal Life: Biblical Coaching for Living and Abundant Life

DRY BONES: Breathing New Life into Petrified Words of the Bible

Table of Contents

Background and History of the Prayer

"Our Father, who art in heaven, hallowed be thy name...*(oh yes, I must remember to pick up some salad dressing on the way home from church)*...thy kingdom come, thy will be done on earth as it is in heaven...*(maybe I should add some croutons and bacon to my list)*...Give us this day our daily bread...*(bread, I forgot bread)*...and forgive us our debts as we forgive our debtors...*(Maybe I should invite Tom and Mary over, but he'll probably want to watch footfall)*...and lead us not into temptation but deliver us from evil...*(it's sad, Fred's not bothering to iron his shirts since Jane died)*...For thine is the kingdom and the power and the glory, forever. Amen... Wasn't that a nice worship service today?"

Words spoken over and over imprint themselves in the mind through the years and become automatic. The words of this beautiful prayer can spill out of your mouth without thinking about what you are saying. Thoughts invade your mind and steal the energy from deep and powerful utterances.

It's not like it's your fault. Sometimes you don't understand the true depth of your own prayers. And yet, when you don't know what to pray for (or what you *are* praying for), the Spirit makes intercession with groanings deeper than you can understand (Romans 8:26). This is true especially when you pray the Lord's Prayer.

Praying the sixty-five words Jesus taught his disciples in a thirty second time span is part of the problem. When you pray it in a group, there's no time freedom to contemplate what each word and phrase might mean. Faithful prayer warriors through the centuries have recommended pausing after each word to give the Spirit an opportunity to teach its meaning and depth. This practice has enriched the Lord's Prayer for many.

Still, most Westerners don't know the depths of the words they utter when the Lord's Prayer is spoken individually or in concert with others. My hope is that I can peel a surface layer away from this masterpiece of prayer so that you might begin to feel the richness of its meaning. Rather than getting too scholarly, I want to open a window and shed some light on what has been covered over by the dust of time.

It's not an easy task to raise a window frame that has been painted shut by repetition over the years. Sudden storms have erupted in churches when a pastor or denomination decided to substitute "sins" for "trespasses" in an effort to pray the Lord's Prayer in the language of today. Some who have opened that window of change have let a tornado into the sanctuary. The vocalized reason is that people want to say it "exactly the way Jesus said it."

I introduced much of the information in this book in a seven-sermon series on the Lord's Prayer. On the final two Sundays, I alerted the congregation that I was substituting an adapted version of the Lord's Prayer into the service for that day. At the end of this book, you'll see I did more than merely replace "trespasses" with "sins."

Thankfully, there was no storm. But after saying the adapted prayer for a second time, I felt the window resist opening any further. "Pastor, when are we going back to the real version?"

I replied, "My sermon series is over, so we'll go back to the real Lord's Prayer next week." Sigh. My plan had never been to permanently replace the traditional version, only to briefly raise awareness and expose some new beauty. It's like trying to replace an old coat someone has worn and loved for sixty years. The "new-Gore-Tex-coat-with-fleece-lining-that's-so-lightweight-it-surely-can't-keep-you-warm" attitude pervades much of our religious practice today.

As I try to raise your awareness to new depths in the Lord's Prayer, it may snatch you the same way the tornado lifted Dorothy out of Kansas in *The Wizard of Oz*. What appeared disrupting and confusing for Dorothy resulted in her leaving a black and white world to enter a world of living color. She began to see things in a new light. Good and bad things continued to happen on her journey. Yet the world came alive with the colors, fragrances, and songs of life.

The good news is that at the end of Dorothy's disruptive experience, the world had not turned upside down. She woke up, still in Kansas, but with a new appreciation for the people in her life. This information about the Lord's Prayer won't be nearly as disruptive to you, but it may start to break loose the dried paint of repetition and tradition. I hope you will be blessed with the new light of clarity and a breath of fresh air as a result.

A Word of Warning

"Be careful what you pray for."

A woman from Alberta, Canada, wrote a devotion reminiscing that the winter of 2003 followed a very dry summer. Hay prices had tripled. She and her husband had to be very careful no hay was wasted as they rationed it to their livestock. Because the winter was harsh, food was scarce and lots of ice made it difficult for deer to find food. She started to pray for the wild deer.

She said God answered her prayers for the deer in an unexpected and unwelcome way. The deer began to eat their very expensive hay. No matter how they covered the hay, the deer managed to get into it. Finally she started praying for God to keep the deer from eating their hay. "How ironic!" she said, "I prayed for God to give them something to eat; now I was asking God to do so in a way that would be of no cost or consequence to me." How many times do we ask God to meet a need that we are unwilling to help with?[1] Accepting that you may be involved in the answer is a necessary component of prayer, even the Lord's Prayer.

Too often, I've prayed the Lord's Prayer with an entitlement attitude: "Give me, give me, give me Lord. Send Your kingdom of peace and joy; send food to meet my needs; forget my unloving actions (and forgive me if I'm too weak to do the same when others harm me). Don't make it so hard for me to do the right things. Keep evil from happening to me. You're so good when You do all this for me. Give me, give me, give me, Lord."

Is this really what Jesus meant? More often than we realize, you and I play a key role in obtaining the desired result, especially when we pray the Lord's Prayer.

First, I'm going to tell you how the prayer evolved over time. Then I'll explore some new meanings in the individual petitions. By the time you reach the end, you will see this beautiful prayer is deeper, wider, higher, and wiser than you could have imagined. Not only that, but you will see that your initiative and participation is necessary in bringing it to its fulfillment.

History

Briefly, this is how the Lord's Prayer came into being the way many churches say it today. In the first century, along the north and eastern Mediterranean countries, Greek was the *lingua franca*, the common language used to communicate between people who have different primary languages. To have a common language expedited commerce in the port cities where shipping and trade was conducted. In the same way, Aramaic was the *lingua franca* of Egypt and most of western Asia.

The books of the New Testament were written in Greek. The Christian witness to the life of Jesus was made available to a wide diversity of people between Jerusalem and Rome. Yet, Jesus probably didn't teach the prayer to his disciples in Greek.

It's generally accepted that Jesus spoke Aramaic. After the wise men from the East angered Herod by not reporting where the child could be found, Mary and Joseph took him to live in Egypt. Aramaic was the unifying language there. We see evidence that Jesus spoke Aramaic in the New Testament. In the garden of Gethsemane, Jesus addressed God as *abba,* which is Aramaic for *father*. When Jesus said you cannot serve both God and mammon, the word *mammon* is Aramaic, and it carries greater depth of meaning than simply money. When Jesus healed Jairus's daughter, he said, "*Talitha koum*" which is Aramaic for "little girl, get up." And the words Jesus spoke from the cross, "*Eloi, Eloi, lama sabachthani?*" are translated, "My God, My God, why have you forsaken me?" This too is Aramaic.

It's also known that there were seven Aramaic dialects in first century Judea, one of them being Galilean Aramaic. That's possibly how Peter was detected as being a Galilean as he stood by the fire when Jesus was being led to trial.

The books of the New Testament were written in Greek, many as letters to individual churches in the areas travelled by the apostle Paul. These letters were passed from one worshipping community to another as the early church grew. There was no "New Testament" until the fourth century when circumstances motivated the church in Rome to establish what would be called its canon—the official documents from which the memory and message about Jesus as the Christ would be passed to all generations.

Jerome then translated the New Testament from Greek into Latin. The Latin version is called the *Vulgate*. Latin became the official biblical language for twelve hundred years—until a few individuals became convicted that the common people should be able to read the Bible, too. The Bible began to be translated into languages that lay people could read and study.

The point I want to make here is that we're already moving beyond the second degree of separation from the language Jesus and the disciples spoke. Aramaic was translated to Greek and then Greek to Latin.

Because of a fondness for abstract concepts, the Greeks tended to explain the world in intellectual concepts rather than in natural, agricultural terms the way Jesus explained them. Greek and Latin are more predictable and fixed in the way they express things. On the other hand, Aramaic is a poetic language, utilizing rhythm, order, and sound to reveal its meaning. Comparing Aramaic to Greek is like comparing a spirited Arabian horse bred to run like the wind with a magnificent Clydesdale bred for heavy work. We'll be moving from a horse that plods along with definiteness and strength to one that is unpredictable and ready to run after being put out to pasture for two thousand years.

Using the Greek and Latin versions, John Wickliffe translated the Bible into English in the year 1382. The institutional church was very unhappy with him. In the end, he paid for his efforts with his life, a martyr for trying to help more people read and study the Bible.

Henry the VIII had more to do with the way we say the Lord's Prayer in English than most people realize. Before 1541, there was no single way to say the Lord's Prayer in the churches of England. After Henry VIII separated from the

Roman Catholic Church, he issued an edict that in brief (and in my words) said: "There are too many ways of saying the Lord's Prayer and we need to all be able to say it in a uniform way, so I want all my loving subjects to say it the way I'm giving it to you right now."[2]

Finally! There was one way to say the Lord's Prayer in every church. No more stumbling over trespasses or sins or debts. And everyone can come to an end at the same time to say "amen." Thank you, Henry VIII.

In 1604, King James commissioned an official English version of the Bible to be written and this led to the way many say the Lord's Prayer today.

When you put words on paper, they begin to set like concrete. If you hear someone say, "If it was good enough for Jesus, it's good enough for me," you know they haven't heard about Henry VIII. And if you really want to say it the way Jesus taught it, you would have to learn Galilean Aramaic.

Roots in Judaism

In the gospel of Luke, the disciples ask Jesus to teach them to pray the way John the Baptist taught his disciples. So Jesus taught them a prayer that sounds remarkably like a prayer the Jews called the "Kadish." This prayer comes out of the teachings of an ancient Jewish sect called the Essenes, a group to which many believe Jesus belonged. The Kadish, as it was translated by Christian scholar Rev. John Gregorie, reads like this:

> *"Our Parent which art in heaven, be gracious to us, O Lord, our God; hallowed be thy name, and let the remembrance of thee be glorified in heaven above and in the earth here below. Let thy kingdom reign over us now and forever. The holy men of old*

> *said, Remit and forgive unto all men whatsoever they have done against me. And lead us not into temptation, but deliver us from the evil thing. For thine is the kingdom, and thou shalt reign in glory for ever and for evermore."*[3]

Rather than the Lord's Prayer originating with Jesus, it could be a version of the way Isaiah, David, and others said it too. That would tie us to praying this beautiful prayer with more saints than we ever imagined—saints that lived long before Jesus.

The Lord's Prayer arose from the Hebrew and Aramaic languages. Like both Hebrew and Arabic, Aramaic has different *levels* of meaning. These languages make no distinction between the body, mind, and spirit. Different meanings of every word are possible because the words are defined by their placement in a system that permits them to be interpreted at each of these levels.[4]

Let me plant a seed with you: As you learn more about the prayer itself, it will show itself to be a universal prayer for anyone who loves and seeks God. One day Christians may be able to pray this prayer in unison with Jews who find value in it. There may be a possibility that together with a Christian and a Jew, a Muslim could pray the same prayer since it draws no doctrinal lines.

I know, I know. That dried paint may not loosen so easily. But I won't get a hammer to jar it loose. Just keep reading and let me show you what I mean.

Translation Difficulties

As I said earlier, the Greek and Latin languages tend to be conceptual, predictable, defined, and black and white in their attempts to communicate meaning. Aramaic is more descriptive, poetic, and possessing many levels of meaning, with words and expressions that possess many shades of color.

Trying to convert words from one language to another is not clear-cut. Translation is not an exact science. Converting words is not like converting inches into centimeters, or quarts into liters. It's not that individual words cannot be explained in another language, but when you cross from one language to another, words lose the social and cultural context that shape how they are used.

Those translations of the Bible that claim to be more "literal" work very hard at matching single words to a word from another language that might mean many things. Instead they create a rigidity that is unnatural. Words tend to develop singular meanings when you haven't been taught they possess literal, metaphorical, and spiritual levels of meaning.

When you consult a Greek or Hebrew to English concordance, you'll find there are several options from which to select as you translate a Hebrew word into English. One example is the word *ruach.* Your choices might be "wind, breath, or spirit." You make your choice based on context, how the word is used in other places of the same document, how the word was used in antiquity, and other kinds of linguistic considerations.

It's important to understand that the choices a translator makes in converting words into another language, especially the Bible, is also dictated by the theology and culture/tradition of the person making the decision. Because there may be several word options to choose as a replacement, one's prevailing theology will often become a determining factor.

> *Every* translation, whether from Hebrew to English, Greek to English, or Aramaic to English, is an *interpretation.*

[Some academics are concerned that the source texts in Aramaic have not been sanctioned as credible by the powers-that-be in biblical scholarship. Much study and research has attempted to authenticate a document that has been dated from the second century, which is earlier than the Greek texts that have been found.

Even if the Aramaic text is valid, words in Aramaic when translated to Greek and English still contain the same historical and comparative obstacles. It has been argued that the English words coming from the Aramaic are closer to the intended meaning than English words coming out of Greek or Latin.]

* * *

These concerns are more for academics and scholars than they are for the person who wants to communicate with the Unseen. The black and white accuracy of what Jesus did or did not say (or mean) in Greek, Hebrew, Aramaic, or the King's English doesn't matter if any of the interpretations in this book assist you in communing with the Divine. What matters is whether a new way of praying the Lord's Prayer helps you become a more loving, patient, generous, kind, and peace-filled person.

Pray whatever words open a path to communion with God. I hope this book will assist you toward that goal.

* * *

This, then, is how you should pray.

~ Jesus, Matt 6:9-13

* * *

* * *

Our Father who art in heaven.

* * *

CHAPTER ONE

Opening to the Lord's Prayer

Click.

I dropped my iPhone into my lap in frustration. I was tired of wading through the multiple choice lists of "press one if you have a question about billing, press two if you want to talk to a salesperson, press three if you want to talk to technical service, press four…"

Why can't I talk to a real person, someone I can explain the trouble I'm experiencing with my telephone account?

My problem was not easily categorized and could not be handled with the push of a few buttons. *Just let me talk to a person who can listen, understand my needs, and then move me a step closer to resolving the issue. And give me someone with the knowledge and authority to make the necessary changes.*

Isn't that what we're looking for when we lift our utterances to the heavens?—someone who will listen, who can get us on the right track and has the power to initiate the changes.

To pray is to admit that someone or something can hear you and is capable of responding. Why would you pray if you didn't think someone was listening and could do something about it?

So *who* are you praying to when you say *"Our Father who art in heaven."*

The Greek word translated as "father" (*pater*) has more depth and meaning to it than the English word allows us to consider. It means "originator of life." In biblical times, the male alone was believed to be the originator of life. Without scientific methods to show both mother and father play a dual role in procreation, they believed the seed/sperm of the male carried the fullness of life. The way we'd say it today is that they thought the male alone provided the complete genetic code from which the embryo developed. The woman was merely an incubator in which the seed of life was planted. Without even considering the patriarchal view of that age, "father" was an obvious choice as the image for the Originator of life.

When children learn about God, they require tangible images they can relate to. My wife and I took our children to a children's museum where they learned about trains and locomotives by looking at pictures drawn on a wall with crayon. We took them to a children's museum in another city where they were able to climb the steps and walk into a restored engine car and caboose. The truth about trains was best learned using an example that they could see, feel, and touch.

The word "father," as a male parent figure, tells as much about God as a picture of a train painted on the wall of a children's museum. It offers a starting point, but that's about all. Tangible objects that have form and substance remove the requirement to imagine what has never been seen or touched before. It's more difficult to understand a concept like God that is not a material object—and is, in fact, inconceivable. Yet we need words, although limiting, to communicate concepts and ideas.

When we were children, our teachers attached a human image to God with form and substance, like a father. Once that picture embedded itself in the psyche, it became difficult to expand our thinking past a human image of God. The process of spiritual maturation requires expanding one's concept of God beyond form, substance, and personality. The image we began with in childhood has to be shaken before we become motivated to move to a higher notion.

Maybe that's why in the Old Testament, the first people of God were called the *children* of Israel. Their concept of God had not moved beyond a material form with emotions and human characteristics. To the credit of the Israelites, they advanced the notion of the Unknown beyond the pagan idols of hand-fashioned wood and stone. The Power in the skies that brought lightning, storms, earthquakes, and pestilence was without form and material substance.

Several Aramaic scholars have translated Aramaic into English in a way that helps us expand the way we think about the Originator of life:

Abwûn

Our Father-Mother,

O Birther! Father-Mother of the Cosmos,

O Thou! The Breathing Life of all,

O Thou, from whom the breath of life comes,

These descriptions might sound uncomfortable to those of us who have been conditioned to call the Creator "Father." They portray an undefinable Creator that doesn't look like a male human. These alternative descriptions start abstract thoughts that require maturity beyond a child's ability to understand. God is inconceivable, beyond form and description.

So *where* is this formless Creator? *Who art in heaven.*

Let's ask an easier question: Where is heaven?

Take a pencil and paper. Draw the waves of a lake or ocean. Draw a seagull flying above the waters. Then draw some clouds in the sky over the seagull. Your picture might look something like this:

Now read this passage from Genesis 1:6-7, *Then God said, "Let there be a firmament in the midst of the waters, and let it divide the waters from the waters." Thus God made the firmament, and divided the waters which were under the firmament from the waters which were above the firmament; and it was so.*

As a child, my less-than-fully-developed brain heard the word "firmament" and I thought—*okay, that must mean something "firm," like land—and it divided the waters from the waters.* Now that I'm older, I've looked up the definition of firmament and found that it actually means "expanse, vault, space." The firmament is the "space" between the waters *under* the firmament—the oceans, lakes, rivers—and the waters *above* that space—the clouds. Another way to describe the firmament is to say that it's the atmosphere around the earth.

That in itself isn't ground shaking until you read the next verse, *"And God called the firmament Heaven."* The seagull you drew is in heaven. Heaven may not be above the clouds. It may be *under* the clouds and *above* the oceans and rivers.

Maybe that's why translators converting the Aramaic words for "in heaven" describe the place where the Creator dwells in these ways:

d'bwaschmâja

Who art above and within.

You create all that moves in light.

Creator of the Shimmering Sound that touches us.

We hear you breathing—
in and out—in silence.

In the roar and the whisper, in the breeze
and the whirlwind, we hear your Name.

You shine within us, outside us—
even darkness shines—
when we remember.

Where ears and eyes awaken, there heaven comes.

Who fills all realms of sound, light and vibration.

The inconceivable Creator inhabits all of sound, light, and vibration. If you remember from your freshman science class, all matter consists of atoms that are vibrating. God is a part of all of matter—a Creator who is closer to us than we imagine…all around us and within us.

The space all around us is heaven? Maybe it is—if we'd just open our eyes to see it.

Often our eyes are not open to the presence of God right in front of us. When the children of Israel walked through the Red Sea, between walls of water on each side, I'd venture a guess that some of the people were looking at their feet and complaining about the mud on their sandals, oblivious to a miraculous parting of the waters. So often we focus on the things that are going poorly for us, our needs that aren't being met, and we miss the spectacular miracles of life that surround us on all sides.

It's okay to imagine God is in heaven. But heaven is not a billion miles away beyond the clouds and stars. God is Immanuel. God is with us. *O Thou, from whom the breath of life comes, who fills all realms of light, and sound, and vibration.* It's a new way to look at heaven and it makes God feel much closer to us than most people imagine. Among us. Around us. Within us.

* * *

* * *

Hallowed be thy name.

* * *

CHAPTER TWO

The First Petition

"Oh, my God! Someone took my sermon notes!"

"Oh, my God! Look at how cute that little baby is!"

"Oh, my God! I can't believe I got an "A" on my math test!"

"Oh, my God! You didn't really say that to her, did you?"

OMG is a short way of writing "Oh, my God!" on Twitter, Facebook, or when texting it.

Many of us are guilty of using the name of God in this way even though there is a commandment against it. In fact, it's one of the Big Ten: *Thou shalt not take the name of the Lord thy God in vain.*

Many people speak God's name like it's no big deal. Hallowed means "to be separated from profane things"—to be spoken of in high regard. According to the writer of Exodus, it's a serious offense and it carries a severe punishment: *The Lord will not hold him guiltless* (Exodus 20:7) as in, "You're going to pay big-time for this!" And Leviticus 24:16 says, *And whoever blasphemes the name of the Lord shall surely be put to death. All the congregation shall surely stone the him, the stranger as well as him who is born in the land. When he blasphemes the name of the Lord, he shall be put to death.*

This is a commandment people break easily, and they rarely say "I repent" after they do it.

Is blaspheming and speaking God's name in vain the same? The short answer is "Yes."

The long answer is that the Hebrew word for "blaspheme" can mean two different things. It can mean *to pierce or perforate*, as in "to put holes in it." Whatever you blaspheme becomes like a bucket full of holes, it can't hold water. I guess that's a literal way of thinking of a holey God—a God whose name has been rendered useless by piercing it with our tongues and absence of respect. From the Christian perspective, humanity literally pierced God with nails in his hands and feet and with a sword in his side.

For both Christians and non-Christians, if you accept that God fills all realms of sound, light, and vibration, there's another dimension to consider. God as sound, light, and vibration includes human beings. It would be blasphemy to put holes (e.g., bullets, arrows, knives, shrapnel, etc.) in any person, for God is within us. The wanton destruction of any moving-form of life is piercing God.

The second meaning of the Hebrew word *blaspheme* is "to call by name." You might have heard that the Jews believed it was a sin to speak the name of God. The reason was because you couldn't speak such an important name with the reverence and awe it deserved. To speak the name of God was to blaspheme His name. The punishment for blasphemy was death by stoning. Twenty-first century secularists have shown themselves more merciful and humane than the God of Moses. They prescribe death by lethal injection so death will be painless.

Some people think the few Muslim countries that continue to sentence people to death for blaspheming Allah are living in the dark ages. They happen to be following the Torah more faithfully than most Christians and Jews (if one thinks a literal interpretation is *faithful*).

One has to ask, "What kind of insecurity does a deity possess who orders the death of his subjects because the Name isn't spoken with reverence?" This, too, sounds more human than divine.

Sometimes people say, "Jesus Christ!" and they don't mean it in the way that puts them on their knees in awe, and worship, and praise. How easily we abuse and pierce the name that is above all names, Jesus, the name at which "*every knee should bow, of those in heaven, and of those on earth, and of those under the earth, ... to the glory of God the Father*" (Phil. 2:10-11).

To blaspheme and to take the name of the Lord your God in vain are both about using God's name in a way that gives it an emptiness of meaning. The penalty is death. This doesn't necessarily mean physical death. It could mean the death that comes when we talk of God so flippantly—a spiritual death. Spiritual death is the loss of consciousness of God's awe and majesty. To speak the Name in a way that is not "hallowed" is to cast it like pearls to swine and reflects a very shallow concept of God's being and nature.

Maybe we need to pray this first petition more intently to consider the majesty, splendor, wisdom, goodness, and beauty of an unfathomable Creator God until we are able to give true honor and glory to the Name.

A person's name is important. I've often wondered *what parent would give the odd names we read in the Old Testament*? Names describe a person's nature. In the Old Testament, people were given names that reflected something about their nature, character, or circumstance surrounding their birth. Jacob means "deceiver." Jacob deceived his brother, Esau (which means "hairy"), and stole his birth-right. Jacob's name was changed to Israel which means "one who struggles with God."

As a child, I was captivated with the descriptive names of American Indians on cowboy shows: Black Hawk, Sitting Bull, Crazy Horse. More recently I read a book of Indian history in the 20th century and came across a name I'd never heard on any television show. An Indian boy's name was "Gets Fat Eating Beef Jerky." It clearly described the nature of a porky little Native American child. Names in Scripture describe a person's nature.

So, what is God's name? What is God's true nature or character? Some people say God's nature is righteous, judge, disciplinarian. The New Testament (1 John) says God is love. That's a good Name to possess.

One of the first commandments was, *"Thou shalt not take the name of the Lord thy God in vain."*

If God's true nature is love, didn't Israel (and all the rest of us who struggle with God) take God's character in vain (render it futile/hopeless/full of holes) by claiming God wanted them to do things that contradicted love? Just asking.

Here are some ways *Hallowed be thy name* has been translated from Aramaic:

Nethkâdasch schmach.

May Your light be experienced in my utmost holiest.

Focus your light within us—make it useful:
as the rays of a beacon show the way.

Help us breathe one holy breath feeling only you—
this creates a shrine inside, in wholeness.

In peace the Name resides:
a "room of one's own,"
a holy of holies open, giving light, to all.

We all look elsewhere for this light—
it draws us out of ourselves—
but the Name always lives within.

Hallowed (honored, revered) be your name (nature) within my heart and mind. 1 John 1:5 says, *"God is light and in him there is no darkness at all."* Jesus said he was the light of the world. Light is a metaphor for knowledge. Maybe at one level, this petition is a request that we might experience the light, the knowledge, the love, the goodness of God in our deepest being to the point where we are so struck by it that we can't help but become holy (which means worthy of praise and reverence). May we grow in our awareness of the true nature of the Creator.

When you possess this knowledge, it will cause you to drop to your knees, without fear but in awe, wonder, praise, worship, adoration, and submission before the greatest power the creation has ever known—Love.

"Let the character of our Creator be lifted to its highest level. Reveal to us that Your name is Love, and fill us with Yourself."

* * *

* * *

Thy kingdom come.

* * *

CHAPTER THREE

The Second Petition

What will God's kingdom look like? For me, the word *kingdom* paints an image from movies that are placed in medieval times. The kingdom is usually a territory ruled by a king, or sometimes a queen. There are castles surrounded by land, serfs, and poverty-stricken villages. Aggressive, armor-clad soldiers on horseback terrify the villagers, taking anything they want in the service of the king. The law is the will of the king who demands complete control, unquestioned loyalty and obedience under the threat of beheading or being run through with a sword. There have been few kings in my memory who were kind, compassionate, and dedicated to the wellbeing of their subjects.

Another kingdom image is the Emerald City in *The Wizard of Oz*. It's probably closer to what many Christians imagine the kingdom of heaven might be like. That's too artificial for me.

Basilea is a Greek word that can be translated as any one of three terms: kingdom, reign, or domain. The *kingdom* of the Creator, the *reign* of the Creator, the *domain* of the Creator. The place where everything functions the way the Creator designed it to function.

What might that look like? What are we asking the Creator to bring to us? Is God's kingdom about obedience to the king's laws where all will be rewarded or punished fairly for their actions?

I can't imagine a kingdom where Jesus reigns looking like my medieval concept. Jesus was humble, merciful, self-sacrificing, and compassionate. In his kingdom, Jesus gives of his own resources and teaches communities to work together to meet each other's needs. No one hurts another person to secure what he or she needs, and the land is filled with joy, peace, patience, kindness, and self-control.

A world in which Love reigns is a place where everyone's physical needs are met. Have you ever thought about what you're going to eat in heaven? Do you think you'll ever have hunger pains? Or ragged clothes? Or no place to sleep?

Love's kingdom is a place where everyone is fed. They receive nourishment in the morning which supplies energy to work during the day. Every child gets a healthy meal so its body, mind, and spirit develop the way they should. They get healthy foods, fruits and cereals that start their day with positive fuel. Adults get their fiber so they are regular and not cranky. Everyone is confident they will receive something to eat later in the day. No one worries how long it will be before they'll eat again or where their next meal will come from.

In this kingdom of peace, many eagerly jump out of bed because they've scheduled time to take a walk, do their yoga or some kind of exercise to keep their bodies fit and healthy. They know a body that is cared for is able to do its best work.

The kingdom is a place where everyone has a place to come home to at night, food, a soft bed to sleep in, and the neighbors do, too. You're comfortable that no one is going to break into your house to steal from you. They don't need to. They have food. They have warmth and a bed.

There are no more drug addicts or alcoholics or workaholics or golfaholics or quiltaholics or bookaholics.

There's no need to buy substances or overindulge to escape the realities of a kingdom where Love doesn't reign. Everyone has easy access to an education and a job; people feel productive and good about themselves. All have grown accustomed to treating each other like everyone has a special gift that helps them contribute to the building up of better parks and cities and schools and communities.

People enjoy working together to make things better. They aren't offended if someone comes up with an idea that is more effective than the one they offered. No one's ego is threatened by the gifts of another.

As the kingdom grows, the prison systems fade away. Those who've served their time for crimes against society have received counseling and training, and they've worked at it because they've been given hope. They have skills that help them to function without fearing their sin against society will drag behind them like an anchor for the rest of their lives. Instead, it's like when Christians gather around the communion table, they hear the declaration that the debt is paid and they are absolved of any residual penalties. The record of each convicted criminal is wiped clean. They are forgiven. No Divine being or human being holds their past sins against them. They are free and know that they will be able to find work. They are once again accepted, respected, and valued for their gifts and creative talents.

When everyone is valued and loved—no one feels the need to pay for physical affection or companionship. And no one devalues themselves to the point where they are driven to sell their dignity or respect so they can feed their children, or keep a roof over their head. Everyone in the kingdom of Love feels secure they will have food, and clothes, and shelter.

In the kingdom, each person senses their value and importance to the unity of a community. Everyone knows that without his or her participation, things may not run as smoothly. They feel needed. But they also know that if they become sick or get hurt, someone else will quickly jump in to fill in so nothing is left undone. They know this will happen because each person has already done it for another. Every individual is confident that if they fall, or fail, people who love them will help them up. No one can imagine that they wouldn't do the same for any other person.

Since no one takes advantage of anyone else, corporations and businesses ask fair prices for their goods and services, prices that adequately reward workers for their efforts, allow for development of new products, and give the consumer excellent value for their money. Corporations work together in healthy ways to spur development of better products and maintain competitiveness that generates creativity and innovation.

Because all are working together with the goal of providing a better quality of life for themselves and for each other, all feel safe and secure. No one fears harm, or loss of possessions, or being disrespected for who they are or what they believe. The only bullets sold for guns are packed with kindness so that if by chance anyone commits an offense, they can be killed with kindness.

When there's no fear, people begin to trust each other. They know they will be treated courteously, honestly, and with dignity. There's no fear of scammers when tornadoes rip through your community. There's only an outpouring of love for those who have experienced loss. People treat each other the way they want to be treated. They value each other the way they want to be valued. They respect each other the way they want to be respected.

Wow. Peace, love, kindness, generosity, self-control, joy, all the fruits of the Spirit being given and received.

Unity and harmony—Heaven on earth. *"Thy kingdom come."*

How do the translations coming out of the Aramaic language describe this prayerful request for the kingdom to come? For me, most of them give a deeper sense of requiring our cooperation.

Têtê malkuthach.

In wisdom, love and equity,
thy kingdom come to all.

Create your reign of unity now—
through our fiery hearts and willing hands.

Let your counsel rule our lives,
clearing our intention for co-creation.

Desire with and through us
the rule of universal fruitfulness onto the earth.

Your rule springs into existence as our arms
reach out to embrace all creation.

From this divine union, let us birth new images
for a new world of peace.

Create your reign of unity now!

The kingdom in which our Creator reigns is one of unity, harmony, and love; people working together as one for the good of the whole. *Thy kingdom come* is not a petition for Day of Judgment to come. Jesus was not suggesting we pray for the last day when time ends and Jesus brings legions of angels to destroy the bad people so the rest of us (the ones God really loves) can live in peace.

My first reaction when I discovered all these variations in translation that come from two words in Aramaic was to wonder how anyone can know for certain what the Bible says just because they know the English words. It might be argued that the Aramaic and English words mean the same thing since God's kingdom is one of unity, love, equity, and wisdom.

But seeing the variations in translation from the Aramaic language helps us understand the fluidity and sometimes indefiniteness of translation and compels us in the 21st century to be less concrete in our claims about knowing what we should expect of God's kingdom and its appearance. The true kingdom may look to people in the 21st century as outrageous as Jesus looked to the religious leaders of his day.

When Jesus began his ministry, he started with these words, "Change your mind (repent)—the kingdom of heaven is now!" At least, the kingdom is now wherever there is unity, wisdom, love, and equity. These behaviors are the proof that God is reigning and the kingdom has come.

Why are we praying for the kingdom of heaven to come when we've been taught to think heaven is where we go when we die? The images we perceived as children need to mature. According to Genesis, the heavens are located between the clouds and the water on the earth. According to Jesus, the kingdom of heaven is now. Heaven-above-the-clouds just might not magically fall through the clouds and descend upon the earth, and everything will be perfect.

Changing my mind about the kingdom of God and kingdom of heaven was one of the milestones in my faith journey. I was forty-eight years old before it happened. I owned my own business and accepted a friend's invitation to participate in a two-year Christian Bible study for businessmen called Christian Leadership Concepts.

The program taught me to start each morning with 30-45 minutes of quiet time devoted to prayer and study. That was fifteen years ago. The practice made such an impression on me and provided such benefit that I continue it to this today. It was during those quiet times that I started questioning what I believed and I began asking, "Why do I believe this?" Most of the answers were "because that's what someone told me when I was little."

To make a long story short, the more I prayed and studied, the more I came to understand and trust God's goodness, and more important – that God *is* love. Once you understand this, the kingdom is near. So near that you can touch it, taste it, smell it, hear it, and see it.

* * *

Thy will be done on earth as it is in heaven.

* * *

CHAPTER FOUR

The Third Petition

A shepherd named John lived with his wife in the mountains of North Wales. One summer morning, a visitor watched as John herded sheep with the help of his champion Scottish collie named Mack. Mack came from a long line of working dogs bred to herd sheep. The visitor watched in awe as Mack circled to the right, then to the left, barking, rounding up a stray sheep here, nipping at a stubborn one there, his eyes always glued to the sheep, his ears listening for the shrill whistle from his master.

When all the animals had been shut inside the gates, Mack raced around the outside of the pens and took up his position at the trough where the sheep would be dipped into a protective antiseptic. When they struggled to climb out, Mack would snarl and snap at their faces to force them back in. Standing next to John's wife, the visitor asked, "Do the sheep have any idea what's happening?"

"Not a clue!" she said.

"And how about Mack?"

She replied, "The dog doesn't understand the pattern or purpose—he only understands obedience."[7] Some Christians, Jews, and Muslims insist obedience is God's will. Sheepdogs can get sheep to do lots of things by forcing obedient behavior on them. But sheep don't follow a sheepdog willingly. They fear it. They run from it. A sheepdog doesn't bring peace to the sheep. The dog's only concern is for obedience.

Defining *God's will* is a major source of religious disagreement. There are at least 613 commands in the Old Testament alone and they're not all good commands. Putting people to death for working on the Sabbath (Ex. 31:14; Ex. 31:15; Ex. 35:2) is a little over the top. The problem with obedience as God's will is this—who decides which commands we should follow?

At this point, there are over 30,000 Protestant denominations in the Christian church because of disagreement. Catholics, Jews, and Muslims have many disagreements within themselves about what to follow in their holy books. The houses are divided and falling. When religion places the focus on commandments and obedience, everyone points at the speck in the other person's eye and forgets about the log in their own eye.

Let's look at what the New Testament teaches about God's will. The apostle Paul said sanctification is God's will for us (1 Thess. 4:3). He explained that sanctification is to possess your own vessel (body) in sanctification (being purified, living a life worthy of praise) and honor. Later in the same letter he said that continual rejoicing, ceaseless prayer, and giving thanks in everything are God's will for us (1 Thess. 5:16-18). To the church at Ephesus, Paul wrote that God's will for us is wise living, and to be Spirit-filled (Eph. 5:15-17).

Peter said, *"For this is the will of God, that by doing good you may put to silence the ignorance of foolish men"* (1 Peter 2:15). Honorable conduct and good works are God's will.

In his letter to Timothy, Paul wrote that we should pray for all people and those in authority, *"that we may lead a quiet and peaceable life in all godliness and reverence. For this is good and acceptable in the sight of God our Savior, who desires* (wills) *all men to be saved and to come to the knowledge of the truth"* (1 Tim. 2:2-4).

Are you seeing God's will yet? Or are you confused?

The last verse gives us a better clue about God's will. Instead of translating the Greek word as "will" like the King James Version does, the new translations move toward meanings that encompass more than mere obedience to rules. Definitions other than "will" in the Greek concordance are "choice, inclination, desire, and pleasure." The definition from Aramaic also suggests a meaning of "deep desire."

God's deep desire is that we live wisely, that our conduct is honorable and filled with good works, and that we are filled with a spirit that is worthy of praise.

Look at these translations that come from Aramaic. They will broaden your perspective of God's will. First, look at the ones that use the word "will."

Nehwê tzevjânach aikâna d'bwaschmâja af b'arha.

Let your will come true—
in all that vibrates (the universe)
just as on what is material and dense (earth).

Thy will be done, as in Heaven so in Earth.

Do you notice something contradictory in these two translations? The first one asks for God's will to come to all that vibrates (terminology that suggests the universe or heavens) just as on earth. The second phrases it the way Christians have said and thought of it for sixteen hundred years—let God's will be done on earth just as heaven (all that vibrates).

I always thought earth was supposed to become more like heaven. Why would a translator think God's will (deep desire) should be done in heaven—like it is on earth? Doesn't God have any control in heaven either?

I ask these questions only to reinforce the new concept about heaven that I stated earlier. Heaven may not be *beyond* the stars. It's the firmament, the space between the clouds (waters above the earth) and the land (waters on the earth). God's desire is not that humans are supposed to act like robots, doing everything perfectly, like the angels above the clouds obey God's every command.

I need you to think a little more abstractly here.

As the Aramaic translation suggests, the universe/heaven is composed of things that vibrate (atoms—all that is unseen) and things that are solid: earth, land, matter. God's deepest desire is that all of creation—air, water, land, living things—would work in harmony, in unity, in peace.

On another level, flesh and blood are solid forms that exist in the space between the clouds and oceans (firmament/heaven). Adam was formed from the substance of the earth. The Hebrew word "adam" means "reddish" as in the color of clay. Conceivably, the "earth" could also refer to *human beings*. Figuratively speaking, *you* are matter that originated from the dust of the ground.

This petition of the Lord's Prayer might suggest: "May your deep desire be done on earth (in our human forms) just as it is done in heaven (all of nature)." In a perfect setting there is harmony, balance, peace.

The Creator's deepest desire may be that your physical body's functions be purified so they work properly, the same way natural systems outside of your body are continually purifying themselves of pollutants. The Creator wants homeostasis, balance and harmony, within your body the same way Nature is designed. Unclean spirits of all kinds can be washed away if you cleanse your systems of impurities, first, by refusing to let them enter your body, and second, by washing with water. Drinking water helps to purify your interior systems by washing out the impurities.

Like I said, there are many levels of meaning that can be explored. If praying this prayer helps you remember to cleanse yourself regularly, inside and out, and causes you feel better, then maybe you will feel like being kind, generous, loving, and patient. You may feel like working with others for the good of all.

Now look at some additional translations from Aramaic that show various levels of meaning that support an expanded understanding of heaven and earth:

Your one desire then acts with ours,
as in all light, so in all forms.

Let all wills move together in your vortex,
as stars and planets swirl through the sky.

As we find your love in ours,
let heaven and nature form a new creation.

Let your heart's fervent desire
unite heaven and earth through our harmony.

The tone of these translations is more of harmony in the natural world, homeostasis, just as nature seeks to find balance.

Another meaning is found on the level of actions:

Help us love beyond our ideals
and sprout acts of compassion for all creatures.

And then, there's another level—the internal dimension:

Create in me a divine cooperation—
from many selves, one voice, one action.

Unite the crowd within in a vision
of passionate purpose: light mates with form.

This is a request for harmony within: Help me get my own act together—let all the voices within me come to agreement so that I become balanced, integrated, and whole.

What I appreciate about these perspectives is that they offer an image of God that is not humanoid in its Being, wanting to control our actions to make us good, and instead, makes me think of an Energy that seeks to bind and unite the world in greater balance and harmony. This Energy is trying to unify all of creation so it works as it was intended—in harmony and peace.

And here's another interpretation:

Create your reign of unity now.
Your one desire then acts with ours,
as in all light so in all forms.

One thing these translations do is encourage each of us to ask questions of ourselves—am I doing my part in working together with heaven and earth? Have I set limits to how much I am willing to give and/or forgive for the sake of others?

The command for Jews, Christians, and Muslims is the same: *"Hear O Israel,* (Christian, Muslim), *the Lord our God, the Lord is one! You shall love the Lord your God with all your heart, with all your soul, and with all your strength"* (Deut. 6:4-5). This is the great commandment. Jesus said a second is like it: "Love your neighbor as yourself."

When we ask for God's will to be done—God's deep desire—everyone's needs will be met. Every man, woman, and child will be fed, clothed, sheltered, and tended when they are sick. There will be peace on earth and peace within the earth (you and me). God's kingdom comes today, one person at a time, one family at a time, one congregation at a time, one community at a time. When the world sees it happen, they will know the Name of the One we follow by our peace, love, and harmony.

They will know we are Christians by our love. They will know Jews are Jews by their love. They will know Muslims are Muslims by their love. They will know Buddhists are Buddhists by their love. They will know Hindus are Hindus by their love.

Lord, let your deep desire be done.

* * *

* * *

Give us this day our daily bread.

* * *

CHAPTER FIVE

The Fourth Petition

Bread is my weakness. The only thing I like better than the aroma of fresh, home-baked bread wafting through the house is buttering a two-inch slice and sinking my teeth into it. Give me thick crust pizza, biscuits and gravy, a hotdog wrapped in a biscuit, or soup in a bread bowl and I'm in heaven. It's easy for me to pray the fourth petition of the Lord's Prayer: *"Give us this day our daily bread."* Yet you probably have guessed there's more to this petition than asking for food.

With the request for daily bread, I'm reminded that the Lord's Prayer is also a community prayer. *"Our* Father*"*, *"*Give *us"*, "Forgive *us* ... as *we* forgive", "Lead *us*", and "Deliver *us*" tell me that I'm not asking only for myself. Even when praying this prayer in solitude, I'm reminded that I don't exist for myself alone. I depend on others and they depend on me.

We can do more together than if we work alone. Let me show you what I mean.

The congregation I serve is helping in a campaign to eradicate malaria from Africa. The first year we asked for donations from individuals, we raised $400. Each family was asked to give ten dollars to provide one mosquito net treated with insecticide to protect several children while they slept. Forty families giving ten dollars provided forty nets.

But when getting rid of malaria became a goal of the community and we worked together at it, a different dynamic came into play. People saw that some were giving more than a throw-away ten dollar bill. Someone decided they had been blessed with health and talents enough to give fifty dollars. Someone else gave one hundred dollars. Someone else gave twenty dollars.

When you work together, you get inspired by the generosity of others, especially when you realize you have greater reserves than they do. It makes you sit back and think, *Is this really all I can give? I know I can do a little more.* The compassion of others helps you stretch beyond the limits you've set for yourself on how much to love. Instead of ten dollars, communities inspire each other to do what is good and right for the benefit of disadvantaged people in the world.

The second year, we spent time developing the campaign as a communal effort. In a depressed economy, the same number of people raised $2,400. People inspire each other toward love and good deeds.

To ask for bread is to ask for the basic necessities of life—food, clothes, shelter. Yet the word "bread" from the Greek tends to reduce the petition to a request for daily needs: *give me, give me, give me* what I need to survive. The translations coming from the Aramaic show there is more depth to the request.

One translation says, *Give us wisdom (or understanding) for our daily need.* Remembering the communal nature of the prayer, wisdom indicates we're not just looking for a handout from the Creator. Wisdom implies more than our collective participation in gaining what we are asking for. It suggests that we recognize how it impacts others around us. Do we really need so much more than our neighbor?

When you pray "give *us* this day *our* daily bread," you are also praying for bread for your hungry neighbor. And when your hungry neighbor is fed, you don't have to worry as much about someone breaking into your garage or home because they are trying to find a way to survive.

More important, the New Testament says, *"... we also ought to lay down our lives for the brethren. But whoever has the world's goods, and sees his brother in need, and shuts up his heart from him, how does the love of God abide in him?"* (1 John 3:16-17).

If communities work together, unified in the purpose of love, we will know each other well enough to see when someone is in need and offer help. That happens at the local level, and then it will spread to the point where we will become unified as a global community. People who are blessed will help those who are not as blessed. Those nations who are blessed will help those who are not as blessed. There are enough resources on this planet for everyone's needs to be met, and more. "Help us bring peace of mind to ourselves and others because we all have food, clothes, and shelter."

Mother Nature continually gives us the opportunity to pull together as a global community as we help those who are in need. Hurricanes, typhoons, tornadoes, earthquakes, tsunamis, malaria, epidemics—we have many opportunities to help our neighbors.

To pray for basic necessities doesn't mean we won't have to exert some effort in order to obtain these things. The apostle Paul tells those who are busybodies and not working, *"If anyone will not work, neither shall he eat"* (2 Thess. 3:10). Yet this is not a blanket directive for all persons. There are many who are unable to work. A disability doesn't reduce one's value to God.

On the other end of the spectrum, for those who imagine they have no one to thank but themselves for the efforts of their hard work, another passage is helpful. *"Do not say to yourself, 'My ability and the might of my own hand have gotten me this wealth.' But remember the Lord your God, for it is He who gives you the ability to get wealth..."* (Deut. 8:17-18, NRSV). To be able to work is to be blessed with health, strength, endurance, skills. If God gives health, intellect, and opportunity—then *"for everyone to whom much is given, from him much will be required"* (Luke 12:48).

Here are some additional options that come out of the Aramaic:

Hawvlân lachma d'sûnkanân jaomâna.

Give us wisdom (understanding, assistance)
for our daily need.

Grant what we need each day in bread and insight:
subsistence for the call of growing life.

Give us the food we need to grow
through each new day,
through each illumination of life's needs.

Help us fulfill what lies within the circle of our
lives:each day we ask no more, no less.

Generate through us the bread of life:
we hold only what is asked to feed the next mouth.

Another interpretation brings it to a personal level:

Animate the earth within us: we then feel the Wisdom
underneath supporting all.

Earth again can refer to the clay from which we are made. That would make it sound more like "Animate my body and muscles to do the things I need to do to provide for myself and my family and my neighbors."

The most basic of human needs is to feel secure. Secure that our physical needs are being met, that we are valued for who we are, and appreciated for the talents we possess. Working together, we provide security for each other.

"Inspire me to get up off my backside, my couch, my 'poor-me' frame of mind and do something that will contribute to the answer to my prayers. Give me a purpose, a reason to get out of bed."

When I'm productive, I feel good about myself. When I contribute to the good of someone else, I feel good about who I am and what I've done. This gives me a sense that I have some degree of control in my life. That's the position I always want to be in. When I'm not productive, I feel guilty, ashamed, dependent, and depressed. That's not the kingdom of heaven. "Lord, let me carry my own weight and then some, please."

It's common for people who've never been on the receiving end of charity to complain about paying the bill for others. But it only takes one accident, one mistake, one blood clot, one natural disaster to transform an independent lifestyle into one dependent on the good health and charity of others. The saying, *It is better to give than to receive*, should remind us that it's better to be healthy, able to work and share our blessings rather than to be in a position where we must rely on the compassion of others.

You and I *are* our brothers and sisters keepers. If I have been given the gift of being able to work, then I am the answer to my disadvantaged neighbor's prayer when he or she prays this petition of the Lord's Prayer.

Another translation from Aramaic reminds me of the Christian practice of Holy Communion. *Give us day by day to partake of Thy holy Bread, and the fruit of the living Vine.* Many Christians understand the practice of eating bread and drinking grape juice or wine to remind us that bread is symbolic of the Anointed One's earthly body (Jesus said, "I am the bread of life") and the fruit of the Vine is symbolic of his blood (Jesus said, "I am the vine, you are the branches").

At another level, bread represents the work of his hands, physical labors of healing, feeding, and comforting others—actions that are the substance of what brings life in its abundance. The fruit of the vine is symbolic of the spirit from which those actions arise, actions motivated by love. When I eat the bread and drink the fruit of the vine in the sacrament, I'm publicly showing that I want his actions and his motivations to come into me so that I might become more like Him, and offer the same to others. This is my goal, to live and act more like Jesus, motivated by love.

* * *

* * *

Forgive us our trespasses
as we forgive those who trespass against us.

* * *

CHAPTER SIX

The Fifth Petition

Many years ago, I went fishing in a place I wasn't allowed to fish. Winter was coming to an end in central Indiana. Snow was on the ground, but the sun was shining and the air temperatures were kissing 55 degrees (F.). I had fishing fever. I knew a lake where there was a power plant that discharged its warm water into it. The water never froze and people fished there year round. So I grabbed my fishing pole, tackle box, fish basket (I'm always an optimist), and boots.

When I arrived, "No Trespassing" signs dotted a line of fence posts, blocking off an area within three hundred yards of the warm water discharge. Obediently, I fished for an hour on the legal side of the fence line and caught nothing. I noticed two people fishing in the forbidden zone. I saw them catching fish after fish. The fever must have made me delirious because I climbed the fence. When I'm in my right mind, I don't do things like that.

For twenty minutes, I caught fish after fish, largemouth bass up to five pounds. But then my conscience overcame my fever and said, *Get out of here, you're sinning...and worse, you're going to get caught.* So I left—with a big smile on my face. But as I drove away, the fever came back and a voice on my other shoulder shouted in my ear, *What are you doing? This is the best fishing you've had in ten years. Go back!*

He was convincing. I went back. This time, the white crappie were biting. Cast after cast, I caught them. As I put my twentieth fish into the fish basket, two men in green outfits and wearing badges from the Department of Fish and Wildlife came walking over the hill. I had to release the fish, received a citation for failing to act uprightly, and paid a fine of $86. I suffered the consequences for my trespassing.

I don't get it. For years I'd prayed to be forgiven for my trespasses. Now the first time it happened, it didn't matter. No forgiveness. I still had to pay the fine.

So what does it mean to "trespass" anyway? When I think of trespassing, I think of going onto someone's property who doesn't want you there—it's an action where you're violating the rights, privileges, property, personal space, or dignity of another person. Another way to put it, you're getting into their bubble—the personal boundaries they've established that protect them from possible harm, whether the harm is real or imagined, physical or mental.

There can be visible signs posted around someone that say, "Don't come any closer." Sometimes you ignore the signs and follow your own agenda. Other times, the lines are not visible and you might be unaware that your actions are perceived as harmful. It doesn't matter if you agree or disagree that your actions are harmful. After all, who was I hurting by fishing a little closer to the warm water discharge? Yet I was trespassing because I had not been given the freedom or permission to be in that space. I had not been considerate of the corporation's lines. Trespassing is stepping over the lines someone else has drawn and it carries consequences.

This petition, coming out of Aramaic, is one of my favorites. It shows us the concept of trespasses reaches many levels. Look at the various ways it has been translated:

Waschboklân chaubên wachtahên aikâna
daf chnân schwoken l'chaijabên.

Detach the fetters of faults that bind us (karma),
like we let go the guilt of others.

Untangle the knots within so that we can mend
our hearts' simple ties to each other.

Loose the cords of mistakes binding us,
as we release the strands we hold of others' guilt.

Forgive our hidden past, the secret shames,
as we consistently forgive what others hide.

Lighten our load of secret debts
as we relieve others of their need to repay.

Erase the inner marks our failures make,
just as we scrub our hearts of others' faults.

A one word explanation of the term "fetters of faults" is *karma*. In the Christian church, we don't use the word karma enough. I grew up with the impression that karma was a pagan word since it's connected to eastern religions like Buddhism. We weren't supposed to mingle with non-Christian belief systems for fear of being tainted by them. Little did I know that I could actually learn something if I broadened my base of knowledge and understanding.

Karma has been defined as the force produced by a person's actions in one of their lives which influences what happens to them in their future lives. What you do in this life will affect you in the next life that you live in a physical form. Most Christians don't believe they will come back, nor do they want to, so they don't use the word karma. Yet if you remove the "future lives" concept from this definition, you can easily apply karma on a Christian level. Karma is simply the consequences of your actions—how your actions influence what happens to you in this life. The consequences can come immediately or they can come days, months, or years later.

If you do good things, good things will return to you. If you trespass or cross some lines where you're not given permission, there's a price to pay. Another way of saying karma is "what goes around comes around" or "what you give out is what comes back to you."

In the Lord's Prayer, we may be praying, "Let go of our bad karma, the things we owe for our poor actions, as we let go the karma of others."

"Remove the consequences of our failures to act uprightly, like we don't make others suffer for their failures to honor and respect the lines we've drawn around ourselves."

Release, or reduce the consequences of what I've done, if at all possible. Have mercy. And teach me to have mercy on others."

Another translation from the Aramaic takes this petition to an internal level of meaning: *Untangle the knots within so that we can mend our hearts' simple ties to each other.*

Many of our struggles are internal. Traumatic events impact our spirit. Things happen to us throughout our lives that we've tied a rope to and won't let the memory of hurt feelings go. Praying this petition, one might be praying, "Don't let that thing I did as a teenager that stepped over the lines in someone's life continue to burden me for the rest of my life."

"Release me from the continual suffering that has come from my poor choices or actions, and help me remove the suffering I may be inflicting on others for the hurt they've caused me."

Or, "Forgive me for not being as good a parent/child as I think I should have been, just as I forgive others for their failures."

"Untangle these knots: help me forgive myself for not knowing any better so I can do better today and feel good about it."

"Release me from any baggage I carry from the mistakes I made when I was foolish, or out of my mind with fishing fever. Don't let these things haunt me anymore."

"Untie the knots within that inflame my emotions whenever I think of what someone did to hurt me."

Each time you think about an event and the hurt it caused carries the potential of tying another knot in the cord. Your mind doesn't know the difference between the real experience and the imagined one. Reliving the event reopens the wound to feel the hurt again. We pray, "Lord, stop me from reliving it so I can move on to the abundant life. Untangle the knots I've tied to this event so I can move forward."

Of course, the best way to avoid negative consequences for treading into the protective space around others is to become aware that others have personal boundary lines that need to be respected. Treat others the way you want to be treated. This is the sum of the law and the prophets. Respect the personal property and emotions of others. Then they won't have any reason to react in defensiveness. "In the same way, Lord, when someone trespasses on my feelings, my property, or my space, give me a merciful spirit that does not need an eye for an eye justice to restore my peace." Your peace is too important to be dependent on what happens to someone else.

Take the time to think about why people act the way they do, and to remember that *hurt people* hurt people. People often hurt others because they are trying to protect themselves. If you can see deeper into a person's actions, you can take their responses less personally. Their actions are rarely about you. It's the knots inside them and what experiences they are tied to that cause them to react in unexpected and hurtful ways.

Let's do something radical right now. Let's untangle a knot.

Open your hands in front of you. To forgive (from Greek) means "to let go." Forgiving hands are hands that are letting go of the failures of someone to treat you uprightly. Forgiving hands are hands that let go of the event that keeps coming to mind and inflames negative emotions of anger or fear or hurt.

In your hands, hold an incident, a conversation, the action of another person, a difficult experience. It doesn't matter if it's a major event or a minor one. What is it that you would like to let go so that it doesn't burden you anymore? Imagine the experience occurring in your hands.

Now take deep breath. Raise your hands and let it float up and away, through the ceiling, up into the clouds. Let it go. Watch it disappear. It no longer exists. Feel a peace as the burden is released. Take a picture of that letting go experience and store it in your mind.

The next time the hurtful experience starts to creep into your mind, don't tie another knot to it. Quickly replace the thought of the event with the image of your hands releasing it into the air. Let it go again...and again...and again. How many times—seven times? No, seventy times seven—as many times as it returns to upset you. The memory, like an unclean spirit, will get weary when it sees it cannot hurt you anymore and will gradually diminish its efforts to come back to haunt you.

Karma. Every action has a consequence. You can build good karma in this life by giving out the fruits of the Spirit:

love, joy, peace, patience, kindness, goodness, gentleness, faithfulness, and self-control. These actions violate no one's personal space. They always enhance the spaces of others and cause them to invite you closer. You will enjoy the karma that comes from these actions: the abundant life.

* * *

* * *

And lead us not into temptation,
but deliver us from evil.

* * *

CHAPTER SEVEN

The Sixth & Seventh Petitions

Every time I drive by a Dairy Queen, I'm tempted to turn in and satisfy a persistent craving to bring pleasure to my taste buds and stomach. What's so bad about that—other than the negative effects of gaining weight by giving in to that temptation? I'm not hurting my neighbor if I eat a strawberry sundae, am I? No, I'm helping a business owner to make a living. I'm helping high school students to make car payments. It makes me happy, and when I'm happy, my attitude rubs off on others and makes them happy.

On the other hand, it could be hurtful to others if I satisfy my impulses too often and gain weight. Too many ice cream sundaes might encourage diabetes, heart disease, joint pain that requires knee and hip replacements. These put a burden on the health care system and everyone pays for people who don't care for the temple in which the Holy Spirit dwells. I may become irritable, thinking I don't look as good as I want. I may get envious of others who place a priority on their health and look great. When I'm envious, I'm tempted to put them down or focus on their faults rather than encourage them for their positive efforts.

But, isn't this stretching the temptation thing a little? There are many ways we justify giving in to the things that bring us physical pleasure. But you and I know temptation is more complex than that.

The problem comes when I'm only interested in bringing temporary pleasure to myself and I'm tempted to forget the needs of others. I forget about the children in Haiti and other countries who are lucky if they get one nourishing meal a day. As of 2014, the cost of one strawberry sundae ($3.95), if given to Trinity/HOPE (www.trinityhope.org) would pay for fourteen meals for children in Haiti; or if given to the ELCA Malaria Campaign would provide two shots to cure malaria in children or pregnant women in Africa.

Do we really have to worry about this stuff? Only if we take the New Testament seriously. I repeat, *"Whoever has this world's goods, and sees his brother in need, and shuts up his heart from him, how does the love of God abide in him?"* (1 John 3:17). I'm preaching to myself just as much as to anyone else.

What about the Aramaic version of this prayer? Can it help us understand anything further about this petition?

Wela tachlân l'nesjuna

Let us not be lost in superficial things
(materialism, common temptations)

Don't let surface things delude us

Don't let us enter forgetfulness,
the temptation of false appearances.

Superficial things: sports, clothing, material success, shoes, cars, golf, fishing, while our neighbor suffers from malnutrition or dies from malaria. I don't think the Aramaic translations are going to let us off the hook. Let us not be lost in shallow, artificial, meaningless things.

This translation places an emphasis on priorities we set for ourselves rather than permitting us to blame the evil one or God for putting something in front of us to test whether or not we'll be obedient. God doesn't tempt us, but we do allow superficial impulses to draw us away from things we ought to do if we love our neighbor as ourselves.

This petition asks for help to do everything Jesus taught in the Sermon on the Mount, *"Whatever you want men to do to you, do also to them, for this summarizes the Law and Prophets"* (Matt. 7:12). There are enough resources on this planet that no one needs to be hungry or cold or to be untreated for sickness. Let us not get caught up in superficial things while others suffer.

* * *

but deliver us from evil.

* * *

The Seventh Petition

Does your definition of evil match Jesus's definition? *"If you then, being evil, know how to give good gifts to your children, how much more will your Father who is in heaven give good things to those who ask him!"* (Matt. 7:11). Does your definition of evil include yourself?

You can find evil everywhere. You can also see evil when it isn't there.

I went to a high school basketball game where the outcome wasn't going to impact my overall sense of security or happiness. I was entertained at two levels, watching the game as well as watching the dynamics of the parents and fans who were highly invested in its outcome.

The teams were arch rivals. Anger and malice swirled in the air long before a foul was committed on the basketball court. There was nothing on the basketball floor that could be called evil, nothing purposefully done to hurt an opponent. The physical skills of players were equal. There was pushing and shoving for positioning, and there were bodies crashing into each other as players chased the ball bouncing around a rim. The deciding factor in the outcome of the game was a result of one team having better ball handling skills, teamwork, and intensity than the other.

However, in the grandstands, this wasn't a test of athletic skills. This was war in rural America. The hometown fans who lost the game said the referees were biased. They magnified fouls by the opposing team. They said the visiting team played dirty. If the visiting team had lost, their fans would have made the same comments.

The home team fans weren't alone in their opinions of their adversaries simply because they lost. Winning the game wasn't a salve for the conquering visiting fans. It was vindication. One mother of the victorious team cornered the young man who played center for the home team when he came out of the locker room and chastised him for being so rough with her son.

Lord have mercy. Deliver us from evil, even when it isn't there.

I was a Little League umpire for one summer. That was a thankless job. It wasn't the players that exhibited evil. Again it was the people in the grandstands. I had to expel one grandparent from the ballpark for acting evil. Maybe sports is evil. It brings out the worst in people.

Lord, deliver us from evil, especially when the evil we imagine is in others.

The only things that bring out evil more than sports are politics and religion. All you have to do is have a different opinion than someone and they think you're evil. No matter what the context, opposing sides see evil in those who would keep them from their goals. When you make your opponents into villains, they're no longer people that you have to respect or love. *Evil* too often refers to our enemies or those who don't think the way we do.

However, in the Lord's Prayer, the Greek word for evil is not the same word that refers to "evil spirits" that Jesus cast out. The kind of evil in the Lord's Prayer refers to things that bring annoyances or hardship, or that cause pain and trouble.

There's a new way to think of evil when you see translations coming from the Aramaic.

But free us from what holds us back
(from our true purpose).

But break the hold of unripeness,
the inner stagnation that prevents good fruit.

From the evil of injustice—
the green fruit and the rotten—
grant us liberty.

Deceived neither by the outer nor the inner—
free us to walk your path with joy.

From the inner shame of help not given in time.

What is your true purpose? Is there something holding you back from achieving it? Is fear of failure driving you to sit in front of the television and holding you back from reaching your potential? Is your own attitude to blame? Is there a voice within you that turns a contest of physical skills into a war of words and emotions? What is your true purpose and what is superficial or false that might be holding you back from achieving it?

Maybe you won't know what is evil in your life until you answer this question: what is my true purpose?

When we pray the petition in community, we have to ask the same question: what is the purpose of our community? You have to know your purpose as a community before you can see what is pulling you away from it. Followers of Jesus might say their purpose as a community is to continue Christ's work in the world – healing, comforting, feeding, casting out unclean spirits, bringing peace, and spreading the good news of the kingdom of God. Anything that stands in the way of achieving those things is evil…like arguing over how much water needs to be used in baptism, or who should be allowed to live in a committed life of relationship, or if the One from whom the breath of life flows wants us to pray with people of other faith traditions.

Praying the Lord's Prayer together, each person is asking to be made aware of how their presence contributes to the community's purpose. Maybe if we could clear away all the superficial things that hold us back from working on our true purpose as the body of Christ, we might get better at it and bring the kingdom to more people. The Church is on purpose when it imitates Jesus. *"Free us, Lord, from those things that hold us back from our true purpose."*

God doesn't put things in front of us to lead us away from our purpose, but we do allow superficial things to draw us away from what we should be doing to love our neighbor as ourselves. There are enough resources in this world that no one needs to be hungry or cold or uncared for in their sickness.

The New Testament tells us we were created for good works (Eph. 2:10). Our purpose is to follow and imitate the One who came to save us. Do you know your role in helping the body of Christ to achieve its purpose? Can you say you're "on purpose"?

* * *

* * *

*"For thine is the kingdom, and the power,
and the glory, forever. Amen"*

or as from the Kadish:

*For thine is the kingdom, and thou shalt reign
in glory for ever and for evermore."*

* * *

CHAPTER EIGHT

The Doxology

By the time you reach the end of the Lord's Prayer, the conclusion may be more like the credits running at the end of a movie than it is a return to glorifying the Source of unity, power, and imagination. Yet if you remain focused in prayer at this point, it too, is capable of enriching your communion with God.

I sat in the sixth row for a performance of *River Dance* in Nashville, TN. A stage had been constructed that protruded into the audience. Its wood floor was at eye level. Amplifiers were positioned so fifteen thousand people in the arena wouldn't miss a note.

I can vividly remember the power and energy of thirty-five dancers rhythmically stomping on a hollow stage and sounding like a hundred drums beating in one accord. I can see in my mind's eye the floor reverberating like the taut skin on a weathered drum, and remember the vibrations that struck my face from the energy of pounding feet. The orchestration of harmonies, voices, instruments, and performance captivated the audience and united us as one. At the conclusion of each song, we jumped to our feet, lifted our hands in exhilaration and released a guttural roar of praise. The blood in my arteries accelerates and my respirations increase today when I bring it to mind. This is what it means to pray the doxology of the Lord's Prayer.

The conclusion of this prayer is called the doxology. It's not part of the Lord's Prayer recorded in Luke's gospel.

Some scholars claim it was added by Christians living in the eastern half of the Roman Empire. It cannot be found in the early official Catholic Bibles, including the *Vulgate* (Latin translation). Yet, the doxology appears to have been part of the earlier Kadish.

I will separate it into segments so you see where various options from the Aramaic originate, and then show where some translations have blended the ideas together.

Metol dilachie malkutha wahaila wateschbuchta l'ahlâm

"For thine is the kingdom"

From You comes the all-working will,

From you is born all ruling will,

Out of you, the astonishing fire,

The Bible claims that you and I are temples of the Living God. Flesh and blood are the domain of God. God inhabits all of light, sound, and matter that vibrates—and that includes you.

The opening of the doxology is an admission, a submission, a Magnificat, a falling on your knees and saying "My heart, soul, and mind are yours to do with as you desire." Yours is the kingdom. "I turn my humble domain over to you, for you are already within me and I will not fight against you anymore. I will work with you."

God is one with us, knits us together, binds us together, holds us together, inside and outside. Where there is division, the binding energy of love is absent and kingdoms fall.

"and the power,"

the power and life to do,

the lively strength to act,

the birthing glory,

This is the "I-can-do-all-things-through-Christ-who-strengthens-me" part of the prayer. This is the place where the initiative to act and become creative arises.

Love is an action word. Love is what moves mountains. Love is the motivation for right action. Love is the greatest power in all the world. *Thinking* about doing good works, and *feeling* like you want to do the right things are nothing without the power that sends your muscles and bones into action.

"and the glory"

the song that beautifies all,

returning light and sound to the cosmos,

What better way to orchestrate harmony than through song? I'm certain that if a group of poets had translated Holy Scriptures instead of theologians, the kingdom of God would have come long ago.

The following are translations that combine the concepts above in a single sentence:

To you belongs each fertile function:
ideals, energy, glorious harmony

Out of you, the vital force producing and
sustaining all life, every virtue

Out of you, the astonishing fire, returning light
and sound to the cosmos

Show upon us Thy goodness,
that to others we may show the same

"forever."

and renews itself from age to age.

during every cosmic cycle.

again and again, from each universal gathering—
of creatures, nations, planets,
time, and space—to the next.

Forever is the recycling and renewing of undefined periods of time as we move closer to the ideal and purpose for which we were created—peace, harmony, love. In faith, one day we will get it right because love will persist.

Amên.

Sealed in trust, faith and truth.

I confirm with my entire being.

Truly—power to these statements—
may they be the ground
from which all my actions grow.

What is your focus and intensity when you reach the end of the Lord's Prayer? Is it pretty weak, more like a period at the end of a sentence or a verbal wave of the hand and "I'm done. I'll see you later?" Is such a weak ending a sign of weak expectancy for future results?

"Amen" does not mean "the end." Instead it directs us to celebrate that God has already begun working on the answer. God knows what we need before we even ask it (Matt. 6:8; Rom. 8:26).

A woman I know lost her husband in a tragic accident. A month later, she was alone praying in a church, asking for direction in her life – what should she do? Her cell phone rang. A pastor who knew she played the organ was desperate. His church's organist had been hospitalized indefinitely. He asked if she felt like she could substitute for the coming month. She knew immediately that playing the organ was part of God's answer. It would give her something to help her direct her thoughts toward the future for a few moments every day. Later she accepted a job as the fulltime organist.

The Spirit knows what we need when we do not know what to ask for. To say "amen" is to shout, "You have the power and the wisdom and the compassion to grant my request, O Lord. In you I hope and I trust."

In Hebrew Scriptures (Deut. 27:15-26, 1 Chron. 16:36, Neh. 8:6, Ps. 106:48), the word "amen" is a declaration of strong agreement with what has been said. A Hebrew lexicon says the proper place of "amen" is where one person confirms the words of another and expresses a wish for the fulfilling of those words. The word "amen" was carried over into Greek and most other languages without being translated into a corresponding word. It remains "amen" across language diversity for all people of faith.

For in Him [Christ], every one of God's promises is a "Yes." For this reason it is through Him [Christ] that we say the "Amen," to the glory of God (2 Cor. 1:20, NRSV).

Paul says "amen" is equivalent to shouting "yes" at the end of our prayers with confidence and conviction and trust. His statement reveals several reasons for trusting there is power and great anticipation when we conclude our prayers with "amen."

We pray "amen" because we know God fulfills every one of His promises, including the promise to answer our prayers. *"Come to me all you who are weary and are carrying heavy burdens, and I will give you rest"* (Matt. 11:28). *"Do not worry about anything, but in everything by prayer and supplication with thanksgiving let your requests be made known to God"* (Phil. 4:6) Just as God fulfilled every promise made to Israel (2 Sam. 22:31; 1 Kings 8:56; Ps. 18:30), we say "yes" knowing the fulfillment of God's promises is founded in is goodness, loving-kindness, and grace.

With every prayer in which we see the wisdom of God's answer, our "amens" become louder and filled with rejoicing. Our trust in the fulfillment of God's promises is confirmed repeatedly. The power of our "amen" grows stronger. We become less anxious about stepping out in faith, and we begin walking into the unknown with confidence where God has made promises.

Jesus told many who brought their requests to Him that the outcome would be according to their faith. Amen" should not be the closing of a cell phone at the end of a conversation with a distant acquaintance. It is a call for the heavens to break open, in full confidence that God fulfills His promises. We shout 'amen' at the end of our prayers because the ultimate "yes" was and continues to be experienced in Jesus Christ.

Amen, Lord! Let it be according to your good and perfect will.[8]

When the world finally recognizes the goodness of the One who desires to unite us, we will dance together as one—in peace, love, hope, in harmony with all—and the inconceivable but long hoped for kingdom will come. Yes!

I hope you will, with me, pray the Lord's Prayer anew from now on, allowing it to envelope you and enfold you in its beauty and spirit.

In closing, on the next page, I have gathered my favorite translations of each petition and combined them to make a version that feeds me in this season of my life.

You might want to go back through the petitions and formulate your own version according to the hunger within your spirit today.

* * *

One adaptation of the Lord's Prayer:

Oh Thou, from whom the breath of life comes,
who fills all realms of sound, light and vibration.

Let Your nature and character
be lifted to its highest level.

Create Your reign of unity now.

Help us love beyond our ideals
and sprout acts of compassion for all creatures.

Give us wisdom (understanding, assistance)
for our daily need.

Untangle the knots within so that we can mend
our hearts' simple ties to each other.

Let us not be lost in superficial things,
but break the hold of unripeness,
the inner stagnation that prevents good fruit.

From You comes the all-working will,
the lively strength to act,
the song that beautifies all
and renews itself from each
universal gathering—of creatures, nations,
planets, time, and space—to the next.

Truly—power to these statements—may
they be the ground from which all my actions grow.

Amen.

Endnotes:

[1] Jean Bonin, The Upper Room Devotional, Nashville, TN (Vol. 77, No. 6, January-February, 2012) 57.
[2] http://www.thenazareneway.com/lords_prayer.htm
[3] Ibid.
[4] Ibid.
[5] Roland Muller, Honor and Shame in a Middle Eastern Setting, Copyright 2000. All rights reserved. http://nabataea.net/h%26s.html
[6] http://www.altalang.com/beyond-words/2008/10/12/ten-most-difficult-words-to-translate/
[7] Adapted, from the sermon "Only Obedience" by Rev. J. Scott Miller from "The Glory of God's Will" by Elizabeth Elliot Leitch in *Declare His Glory Among the Nations*, pp. 129-130 (found in sermons.com, John 10:1-21).
[8] Adapted from my article, "Claim the Power of Amen" written for *Pray!* magazine, 2008.

Study Questions

1. When did you learn to pray the Lord's Prayer?

2. How often do you say the Lord's Prayer when you are alone? When you pray it with others, does it have different feeling?

3. Have you ever prayed the Lord's Prayer a single word at a time so that you were able to think deeply about each word and phrase? How would this make a difference? What prevents you from attempting it?

4. Why is it hard for people to change something they've thought or done for decades? Is there something they fear?

5. What are the benefits of repetition and tradition? What are the negatives?

6. Have you considered that you might be involved in achieving the answer to your prayer when you pray the Lord's Prayer?

7. Where does God/the Spirit that we pray to dwell? (John 14:16-17; Romans 8:9-11; 2 Cor. 13:5; Eph. 3:14-20; Phil. 2:13; Col. 3:8-11; 2 Tim. 1:14; 1 Jn. 3:24; 1 Jn. 4:13).

8. What evidence is there to know that Jesus spoke Aramaic?

9. Why is it an imperfect process to translate from one language to another?

10. If the Lord's Prayer originated with the Essenes, an ancient Jewish sect, what prevents Christians from praying it side by side with Jews?

11. The Quran agrees that the Hebrew Scriptures are God's word and are to be followed. Does this bring us closer to being able to pray a similar prayer with Muslims? Would it help our interactions with other faith traditions to think we are praying to the same, the only, God who created life?

(Has it helped the interactions of varied denominations in Christianity to understand that we pray to the same Creator?)

Opening to the prayer – *"Our Father who art in heaven."*

1. There is growing momentum for changing the word that refers to God as "Father" to something more generic – why is that upsetting to some people? Is it more accurate?

2. If the Greek word *pater* (translated as *father*) refers to the ultimate originator of life, did Jesus encourage people to imagine God as a super powerful human image (John 4:24)?

3. Some of the descriptions of the One we are praying to in the Lord's Prayer sound "new age." This label seems to give a plastic or negative undertone in the minds of traditional Christians. Is this an accurate connotation?

4. Which Aramaic description helps you to expand your image of the Originator of life?

5. Where did your current picture of heaven come from?

6. If the Originator of life is in heaven, what does heaven look like, according to Genesis 1:6-8?

7. When Jesus said, "Repent. The kingdom of heaven is at hand," what do you think he meant?

   (Hint: the Greek word definition for repent is "change your mind" – not "feel remorseful.")

8. If you believed that heaven is the earth's atmosphere and Jesus is going to come through the clouds on the Last Day, this might mean all who believe in His name will live on earth. Who do you think is going to pave the roads in gold…His legions of angels? Or will you and I have to do the work? Will Jesus work a miracle and make all things look like the picture in Revelation 21:10-26?

9. Would it change the way you treat the environment today if you knew you were coming back to earth to spend eternity?

10. How could it be "good news" that the kingdom of heaven *is* at hand?

First petition – *"Hallowed be thy name."*

1. If people are forbidden to take God's name in vain the same way they are forbidden not to kill or to commit adultery, why do so many Christians ignore this command – even though it's one of the "big ten" commandments?

2. Make a list of negative consequences that result from taking God's name in vain.

3. Do you know anyone that was put to death for taking God's name in vain? Why is the punishment in the Old Testament so severe (Lev. 24:16)? Why don't we enforce it today?

4. Are there any places in the New Testament where God prescribes death for specific sins?

5. What's so bad about treating God's name in a way that it has holes in it?

6. What does your name mean? Why was it given to you?

7. Do you bear anyone else's noble name (James 2:7)? Do you put holes in that name by your words or actions?

8. What name do you call God by? What is your idea of God's true nature?

9. What part do you play in hallowing God's name?

10. Which Aramaic translation helps you develop a greater reverence for God's name?

Second petition – *"Thy kingdom come."*

1. When the Creator's kingdom comes, what do you think it will look like?

2. Why doesn't the world look like that now?

3. What do you think it means that the Son of Man will come on the clouds of heaven (Matt. 24:30)?

4. Do you accept that you have a part to play in bringing the kingdom into being?

5. What kind of changes might you make in your life that will help the kingdom of God to come?

6. Why is it so difficult to picture a world in which everyone loves and cares for each other, where everyone's needs are met? Where should it start?

7. How do the Aramaic translations encourage us to work together to help the kingdom to come?

8. How might you prepare the soil of your heart and mind so that you might be open to changing your mind about some of the concepts of God, the kingdom, and heaven that were given to you by others?

Third petition – *"Thy will be done on earth as it is in heaven."*

1. Why do you think there are so many Protestant denominations?

2. What was Jesus' prayer in John 17:11? Are we any closer to this goal – why or why not?

3. At this point, most Christians don't think it is God's will for us to put blasphemers, adulterers, disobedient children, Sabbath-breakers to death. Does the New Testament give us a clear understanding of God's will? (1 Thess.4:3; 5:16-18; Eph. 5:15-17; 1 Peter 2:15; 1 Tim. 2:2-4)

4. What do you think is God's will?

5. If the firmament, the earth's atmosphere, is "heaven" – then how are we to understand God's will being done on earth as in heaven, or in heaven as on earth?

6. Why isn't the Bible more clear, more concrete, so we might understand it readily?

7. Is there anything in this petition that relates to the petition before it?

8. How would you act differently if you believed you have a part to play in God's deepest desire being done?

Fourth petition – *"Give us this day our daily bread."*

1. When you say the words of the Lord's Prayer, do you feel yourself praying for the community or only for yourself? How is the prayer about community?

2. Why is it important to expand the prayer beyond praying for self only?

3. How does working together inspire us to help the kingdom to come?

4. What does "bread" mean beyond food?

5. Could there be a spiritual meaning beyond meeting the needs of the body (John 6:48)? How might Jesus be seen as the sustenance for life?

6. How are you to play a part in giving *us* this day our daily bread (1 John 3:16-17)?

7. Some people credit God's punishment as the reason for disasters in the world. How could disasters be seen in a more positive light?

8. Talk about the way many Christians use Scripture to avoid helping their neighbor in need (2 Thess. 3:10), and then contrast it with Deut. 8:17-18 and Luke 12:48.

9. How do the Aramaic translations allow a broader understanding that teaches you and I are participants in receiving the answer to our own prayer?

10. When (or why) is it better to give than to receive?

Fifth petition – *"Forgive us our trespasses as we forgive those who trespass against us."*

1. When have you trespassed? Were there any specified consequences? Were they enforced? If you weren't caught, were there "other" consequences?

2. What's worse – trespassing or getting caught?

3. We pray for God to forgive our trespasses. We complain when people or corporations make us pay a penalty for our indiscretions. Yet in the Lord's Prayer, we ask for help to be more forgiving when people go against our wishes. Where do you draw the line between forgiving and helping someone to recognize the importance of avoiding the consequences of their actions in the future?

4. Have you ever let go of imposing negative consequences on someone, even though you thought they were justifiable, when someone harmed you? What happened?

5. How do the Aramaic translations expand your understanding of what it means to forgive?

6. What is meant by "fetters of faults"? Give some examples of "fetters of faults." What are you asking God to release at this level of meaning? Is this fair?

7. We often think of forgiveness as coming only from the one who has been violated. How can forgiveness be something that happens within the trespasser?

8. Where is justice a concept that is "of the world" (Ex. 21:23-25)? Is this Jesus's kind of justice (Matt. 5:38-41)?

9. How can a person's single trespass require forgiveness seventy times seven times (Matt. 18:21-22)?

10. How might you begin to develop good karma?

Sixth & Seventh petitions – *"And lead us not into temptation, but deliver us from evil."*

1. Where do you draw the line between enjoying the abundant life God intended for creation and wallowing in guilt for eating a strawberry sundae—when you know someone else is starving?

2. Why did Jesus teach his disciples to pray that the "Father" not lead us into temptation when the book of James says, "God does not tempt us" (James 1:13)?
3. When thoughts enter your mind and tempt you to do something that would harm your neighbor, is that sin?

4. Who defines what is "superficial" and what isn't?

5. Do you consider yourself "evil" (Matt. 7:11)? Do you need to be delivered from yourself?

6. When might you see "evil" and it isn't there? What makes you classify things as "evil" when they themselves are not bad? Where does evil come from (Mark 7:21)?

7. Is there a connection between superficial things and what comes out of the heart (Matt. 6:19-21; Luke 12:32-34)?

8. How might evil be related to things that hold you back from achieving your true purpose in life?

9. How do you determine your true purpose? What does Paul think is your purpose – do you agree? (Eph. 2:10)?

10. Are you "on purpose" today?

Doxology – *"For thine is the kingdom…Amen!"*

1. The end of a good book or movie requires a powerful conclusion so you walk away energized and motivated to act. Are you ever motivated to act when you reach the end of the Lord's Prayer? What part do you play in allowing the ending of the prayer to do its work?

2. Fire in the Bible is often symbolic of purification and passion rather than punishment. How is God an astonishing fire? Where is this Fire located (1 Cor. 3:16-17)?

3. What is supposed to be the power behind all actions for those who love God (1 John 4:7-8)? In the Gospel of John, Jesus told the Pharisees (five times) that they did

not know God. How does this Bible verse help to explain what he meant?

4. Can you say you know God (based on the criterion in 1 John 4:7-8)? Does that power come from within you or from outside of you?

5. How is the word "amen" used in Deut. 27:15-26; 1 Chron. 16:36; Neh. 8:6; Ps. 106:48?

6. What does "amen" express in 2 Cor. 1:20? Is this your sentiment when you end your prayers?

7. When you look at the prayer phrase by phrase, can you see how the translations from Aramaic can be recognized in the traditional English?

8. In the newer options, does there appear to be one or two common themes?

9. Go through the options for each petition and build a prayer from the Aramaic/English phrases that fit with your life and needs today.

* * *

Information about the author:

Paul W. Meier received a Masters of Divinity degree from Vanderbilt Divinity School and a Masters of Sacred Theology from Lutheran Theological Southern Seminary. He is a second career Lutheran pastor who has been published in The Upper Room, Christ In Our Home, Pray!, Alive Now, The Lutheran, and Lutheran Partners.

Other books by Paul W. Meier

The Beatitudes:
Finding New Meanings in the Language Jesus Spoke

Praying the Gospels with Martin Luther:
Finding Freedom in Love

How to Love the Lord Your God
With All Your Heart and Change Your Life Forever

30 Days To Loving God With All Your Heart

The Kingdom of Heaven Begins Today

Divorce and Remarriage:
Biblical Proof in Favor of Compassion

The ANCIENT Understanding of Eternal Life:
Biblical Coaching for Living and Abundant Life

DRY BONES:
Breathing New Life into Petrified Words of the Bible

Made in the USA
San Bernardino,
CA

59111443R00055